AF228527

THE WORLD'S MOST VILE
Vampires

A&D Xtreme
BOLD HI-LO NONFICTION
An imprint of Abdo Publishing
abdobooks.com

S.L. HAMILTON

TAKE IT TO THE XTREME!

GET READY FOR AN XTREME ADVENTURE!
THE PAGES OF THIS BOOK WILL TAKE YOU INTO THE THRILLING
WORLD OF THE VILEST VAMPIRES ON EARTH.
WHEN YOU HAVE FINISHED READING THIS BOOK, TAKE THE
XTREME CHALLENGE ON PAGE 45 ABOUT WHAT YOU'VE LEARNED!

ABDOBOOKS.COM

Published by Abdo Publishing, a division of ABDO, PO Box 398166, Minneapolis, Minnesota 55439. Copyright © 2022 by Abdo Consulting Group, Inc. International copyrights reserved in all countries. No part of this book may be reproduced in any form without written permission from the publisher. A&D Xtreme™ is a trademark and logo of Abdo Publishing.

Printed in the United States of America, North Mankato, MN.

032021

092021

THIS BOOK CONTAINS
RECYCLED MATERIALS

Editor: John Hamilton; Copy Editor: Bridget O'Brien

Graphic Design: Sue Hamilton

Cover Design: Laura Graphenteen; Cover Photo: Shutterstock

Interior Photos & Illustrations: Alamy-pgs 4-5, 8-9 & 17; American International Pictures-pg 41 (bottom); Angus McBride-pg 31; AP-pg 29; Bantam Books-pg 37 (right); British Library-pg 7; Chermol & Fishman-pg 33; Focus Home Interactive-pg 42 (bottom); Gold Key Comics-pg 38 (top); iStock-pgs 22-23, 26, 27 & 29 (inset); Jean-Pierre Dalbéra-pg 25; Konami-pg 42 (top); Marvel Comics-pgs 38 & 39; Minden-pgs 34-35; National Geographic-pg 32; P. Burne-Jones-pg 6; Paradox Interactive-pg 43; Shutterstock-pgs 10-15, 19 (inset), 20-21, 36-37 (bkgrd), & 44; Skyhigh Publications-pg 37 (left); Sony Pictures Animation-pg 41 (top); Spirits of the Philippine Archipelago/Mildly Interesting Drawings-pg 18-19; Universal Pictures-pgs 28 & 40; University of California-Berkeley-pg 35 (inset); Wikimedia-pg 30; William Bartlett Ed.-pg 36 (inset); Wu Wai-cheung-pg 24.

LIBRARY OF CONGRESS CONTROL NUMBER: 2020948033

PUBLISHER'S CATALOGING-IN-PUBLICATION DATA

Names: Hamilton, S.L., author.

Title: The world's most vile vampires / by S.L. Hamilton

Description: Minneapolis, Minnesota : Abdo Publishing, 2022 | Series: Xtreme screams | Includes online resources and index.

Identifiers: ISBN 9781532194887 (lib. bdg.) | ISBN 9781644946268 (pbk.) | ISBN 9781098215194 (ebook)

Subjects: LCSH: Vampires--Juvenile literature. | Vampires in popular culture--Juvenile literature. | Vampires in mass media--Juvenile literature. | Vampires on television--Juvenile literature. | Vampires in literature--Juvenile literature. | Monsters--Juvenile literature

Classification: DDC 398.2454--dc23

TABLE OF
Contents

CHAPTER 1

THE WORLD'S MOST VILE
Vampires

A vampire is a **vile**, supernatural creature with legendary powers. **Myths** tell of the **undead** arising from their coffins at night. A vampire's sharp fangs pierce human skin to drink the blood of its prey.

5

History

Most vampire history comes from Eastern European stories. However, people and cultures all over the world have tales of vampires and vampire-like creatures.

Stories of a nighttime, vampire-like creature called the bogey-owl were told in the late 1800s.

An illustration from 1893 shows a gathering of vampires and demons.

Many European legends say vampires turn into bats. However, there are other tales that claim vampires can become rats, owls, moths, foxes, or wolves.

CHAPTER 3

HOW TO TELL IF SOMEONE IS A
Vampire

Vampires are neither alive or dead. They are something in-between. Because they are not alive, vampires do not have a heartbeat. They cannot be hurt by bullets or swords. Some legends say they do not have reflections.

Long, unnatural fangs are a way to tell if someone is a vampire. Most stories also say that vampires may only come out at night. Other tales say that vampires simply must stay out of the sunlight.

XTREME FACT

Because vampires are humans who have died and not gone to the afterlife, they are considered unholy. Christian items, such as a cross or holy water from a church, may burn a vampire.

CHAPTER 4

BECOMING A Vampire

The most common way to become a vampire is from the bite of another vampire. Some **myths** say a victim becomes a vampire right away. Sometimes, it takes a few days. Other tales say that a vampire needs to feed at least three times before the victim becomes a vampire.

XTREME FACT
Vampire victims are usually bitten in the neck.
This is because the neck's carotid artery is one
of the largest blood vessels in the body.

There are also stories of spells or **talismans** that may change a human into a vampire. People born during full moons or into **cursed** families may become **undead**. Drinking one's own blood mixed with a few drops of a vampire's blood might make someone supernatural.

Vampire Sightings

In Austria, a vampire called a mara takes the shape of a horse. The horse vampire can control people's minds while they sleep. This is where we get the term nightmare.

The mara sat on a victim's chest, making it difficult to breathe.

Mara

In the Philippines, there are stories of a vampire witch called an aswang. The aswang is not dead but is a living person (usually a woman) who transforms herself into a bird or a bat. She hides in trees, waiting to drink the blood of people who are too sleepy or sick to fight back.

An aswang was said to drink blood from a person's neck, arm, or ankle.

Scotland is the home of blood-drinking fairies called glaistigs. They take the form of beautiful women. Men are unable to resist their call, but they pay a terrible price: the glastigs lure them into swamps and drink their blood.

Some legends say a glaistig has the top half of a woman and the bottom half of a goat.

The only way to defeat an
aptrgangr is to wrestle it
and win, and then force it
back into its grave.

In Iceland, people who live close to cemeteries are afraid of the aptrgangr. The word means "one who walks after death." These creatures have immense strength. The aptrgangr devours its victims or drinks their blood. The victim becomes an aptrgangr, too.

A spell written on paper is placed on a jiangshi's forehead to stop it. But if the paper blows off, the jiangshi can move again.

Jiangshi (pronounced chong-shee) are the dreaded hopping vampires of China. They drink the blood or suck the life force out of their victims. The jiangshi are people who did not get a proper burial in their hometown. But because they are dead, they can't move, so they must hop back to their hometown for burial.

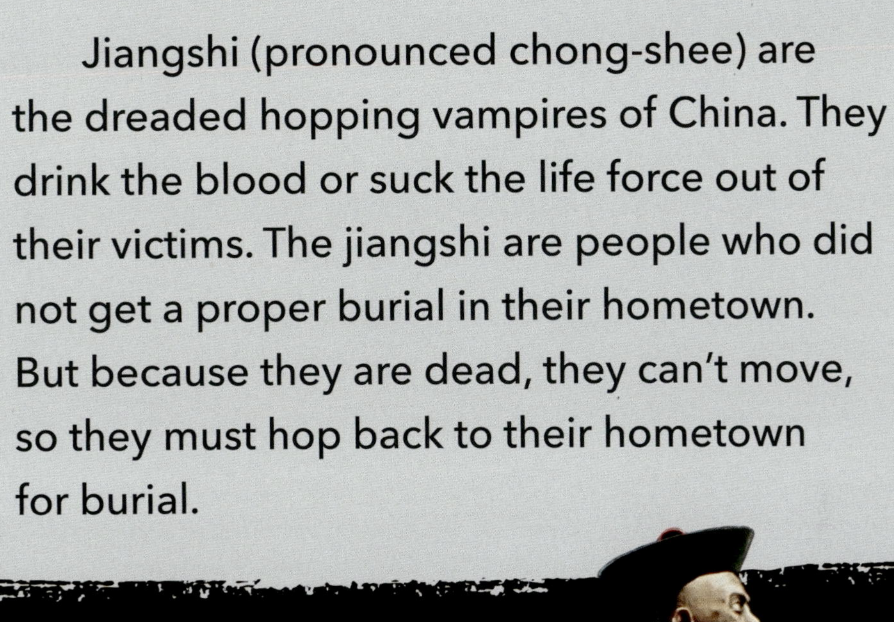

Jiangshi means "stiff corpse" in Chinese.

CHAPTER 6

HOW TO
Kill a Vampire

The easiest way to end a vampire's life is to expose the sleeping monster to sunlight. Legends say that the **undead** must lie in their coffins in a layer of dirt from their homeland during the day. If sunlight hits them, they burst into flames.

The most common way to kill a vampire is to drive a wooden stake through its heart. In times past, people sometimes cut off the head of a corpse, or put a clove of **garlic** in its mouth to prevent vampirism. Garlic is said to keep vampires away. It doesn't kill them, but they do not like it.

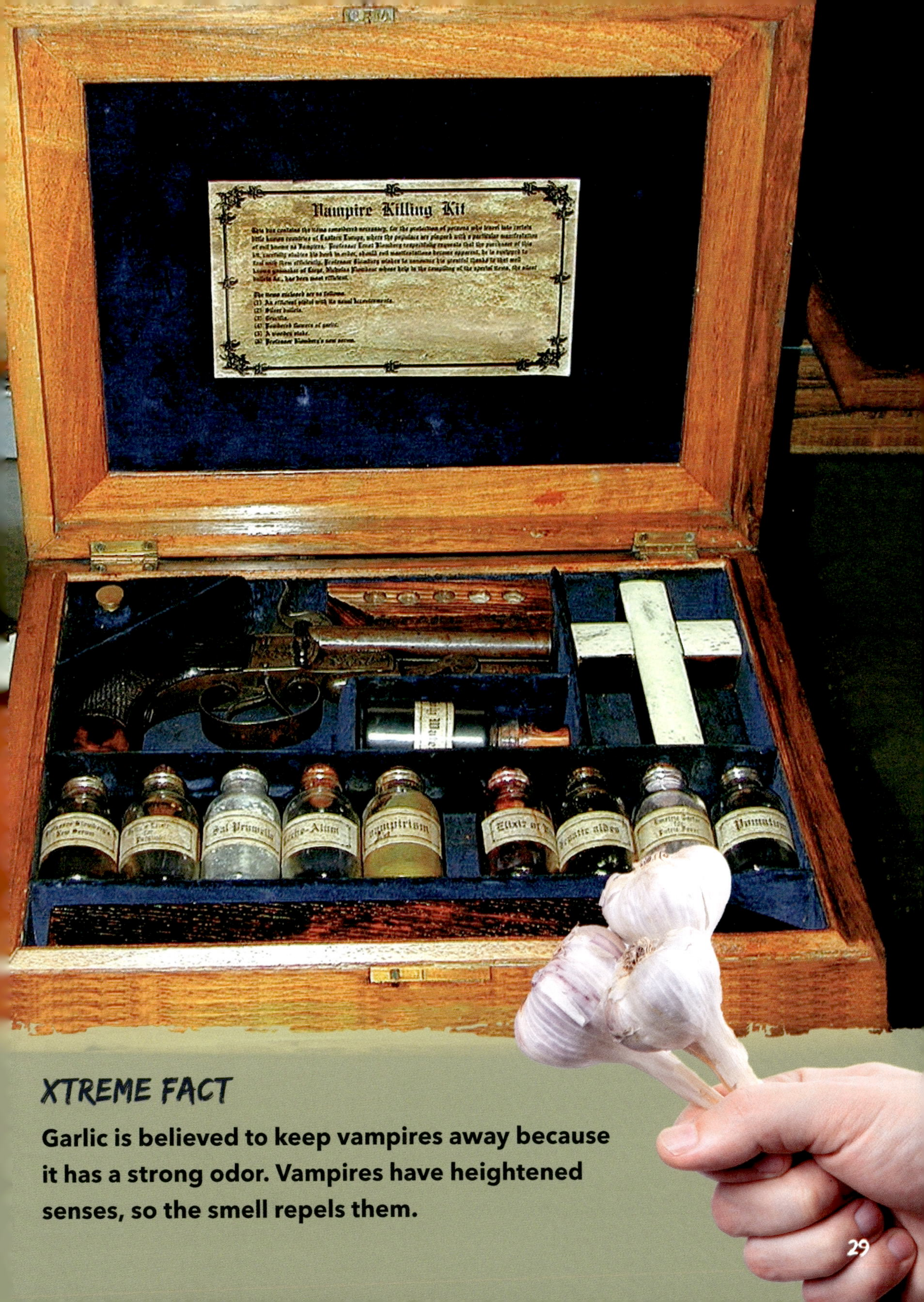

XTREME FACT

Garlic is believed to keep vampires away because it has a strong odor. Vampires have heightened senses, so the smell repels them.

Real Vampires

Vlad Dracula was a real person. He was the prince of Walachia, within today's country of **Romania** in Eastern Europe. He ruled in the late 1400s.

Dracul means "dragon." Vlad got this name from savagely defending his land against invading armies. Dracula tortured and killed thousands of foreigners and countrymen who disrespected him. However, there are no stories of him actually drinking blood.

XTREME FACT

Dracula was also called Vlad the Impaler because he had his enemies killed by impaling them on large stakes set in the ground.

Sometimes people dug up a grave to see if a person had become a vampire. When a body **decomposes**, the lips and gums **recede**, revealing long teeth. People saw long "fangs" and believed the dead person was a vampire.

A mummy's face shows how a person's lips and gums dry up, revealing long teeth.

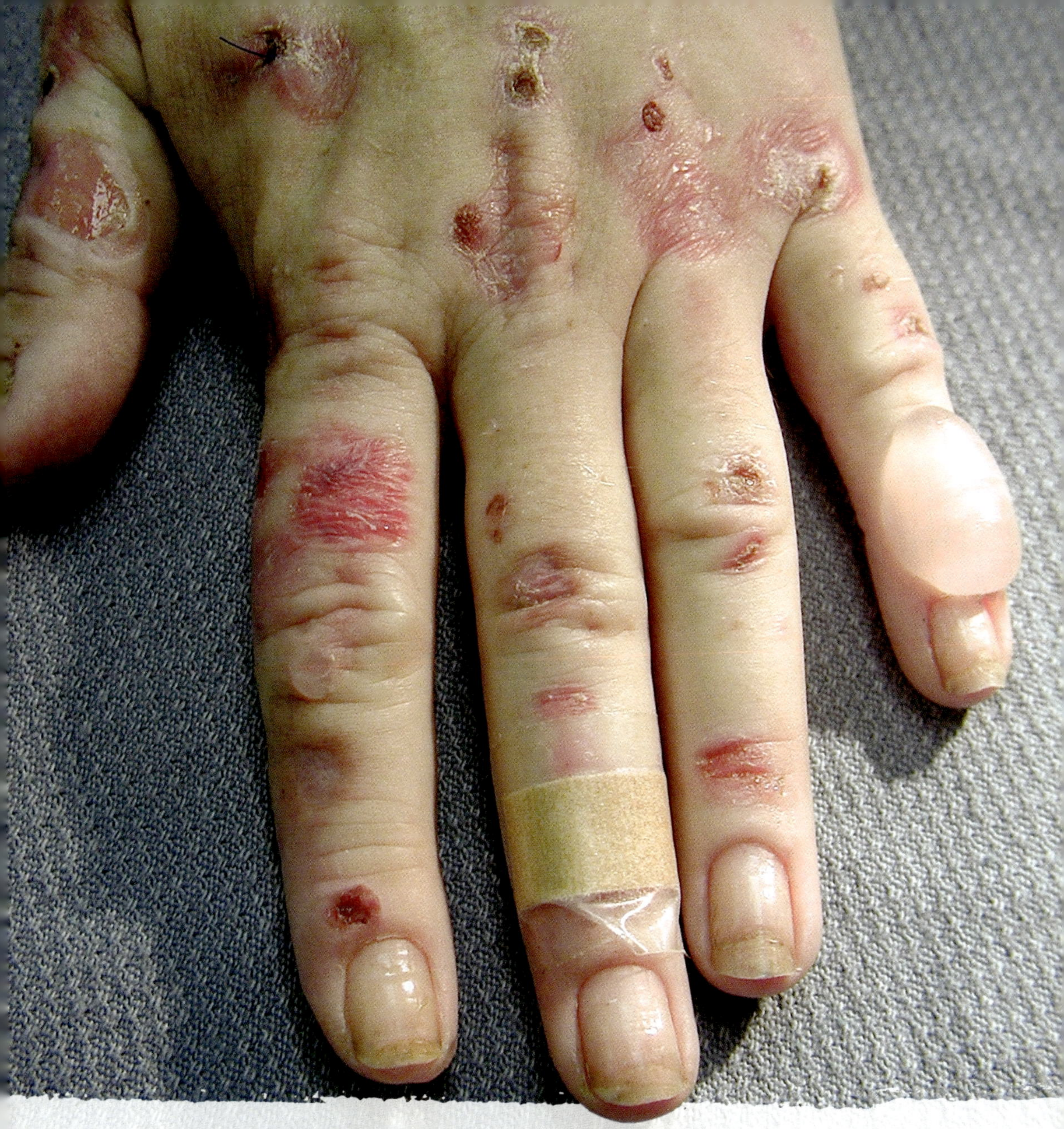

A rare disease called cutaneous porphyria makes the sufferer very sensitive to sunlight. When exposed to the Sun, the skin will blister, swell up, or get red. There is no cure. People with this condition must avoid sunlight, only coming out at night.

Being bitten or scratched by an infected bat is the leading cause of human rabies deaths in the United States.

Rabies can be contracted by a bite from a rabid animal, including bats. If untreated, rabies kills. People become confused and see things. They may have too much saliva. A watery froth can appear on their lips and appear bloody. Vampire folklore may have come from a person suffering from rabies.

Rabies must be treated within 2-10 days of a person having contact with an infected animal. Without the vaccine, the disease is almost always fatal. A victim's symptoms may look like vampirism.

CHAPTER 8

VAMPIRES
In the Media

Vampires are the subject of thousands of books, movies, and games. The most famous vampire tale came from author Bram Stoker. He published *Dracula* in 1897. The book is written in the form of letters and diary entries. His **fictional** tale seems real.

In Bram Stoker's tale, Count Dracula leaves his castle in Transylvania and goes to England. There he faces vampire hunters led by Professor Van Helsing.

The Vampyre: A Tale is thought to be the first vampire novel. It was written by John William Polidori in 1819. Thousands of stories of powerful creatures who feast on blood have followed, including tales by such famous authors as Stephen King and George R. R. Martin.

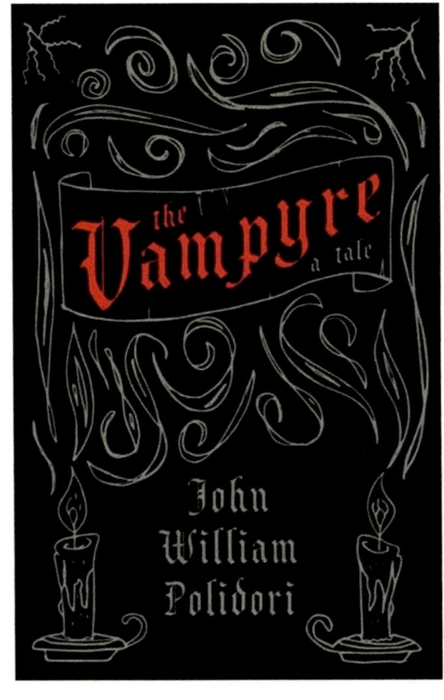

Polidori's *The Vampyre: A Tale* is the story of a vampire whose attention brings death.

Martin's *Fevre Dream* tells the tale of a riverboat captain and a vampire traveling the Mississippi River.

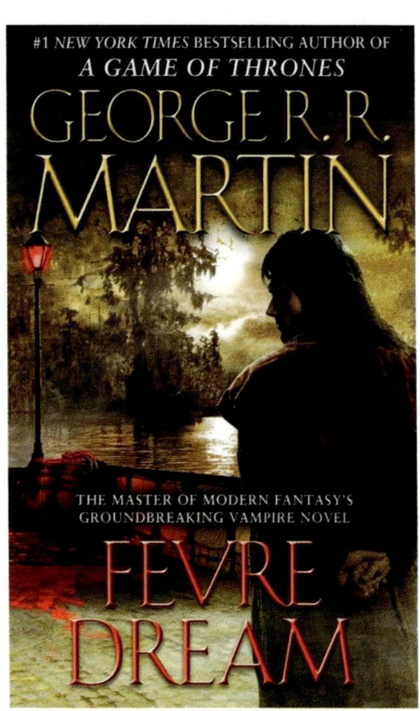

Vile vampires are popular in comic books. But in 1954, the Comics Code Authority was formed to make comics less terrifying. The code forbade using vampires. Vampires did not come back until the 1960s. They first appeared as funny characters and later in frightening form.

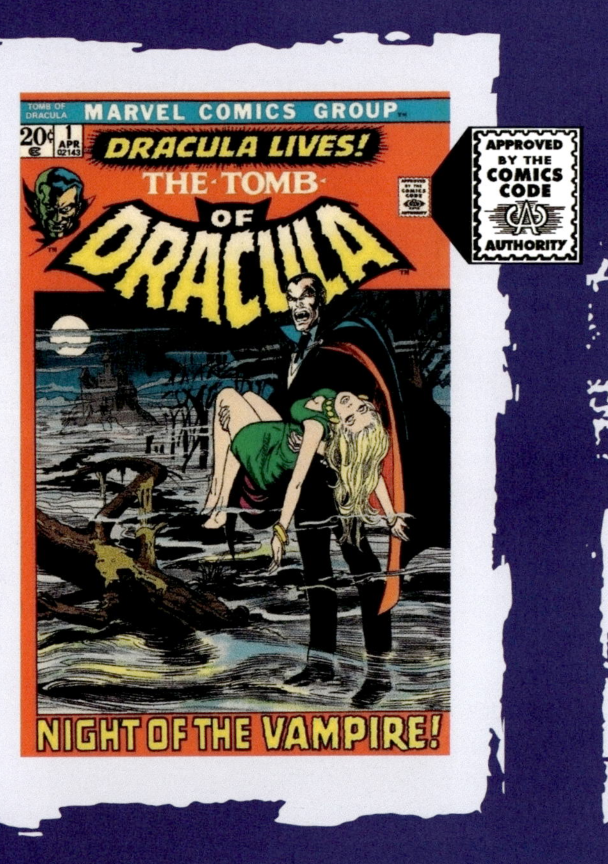

Once the Comics Code Authority relaxed their control over vampire stories, comic book publishers began creating frightening vampire adventures again. Marvel Comics developed series such as *The Tomb of Dracula, Morbius: The Living Vampire*, and *Blade*.

STRANGE TALES
From MARVEL
DEC
#3
BLADE
McGREGOR
HAGAN
FLOREA

Movies of vampires and their slayers have been made for more than a century. Most are frightening, but some are animated films and comedies.

XTREME FACT

Before 1931's *Dracula* was released, the studio started a rumor that the movie was so scary, people had fainted in the theater. People packed theaters to see this terrifying, and successful, film.

Above: Count Dracula runs a hotel in the animated *Hotel Transylvania* series.
Below: Dracula is a disco dancer in New York City in 1979's *Love at First Bite*.

Castlevania is a series of games that first came out in 1986. Players hunt vampires and other supernatural creatures.

In *Vampyr*, gamers play Jonathan Reid, a London doctor turned into a vampire, who must either kill, or control his bloodlust.

Vampires, both as good and evil characters, are often featured in video games. Some games allow players to hunt vampires, some have gamers playing the vampire, while others have vampires fighting other vampires.

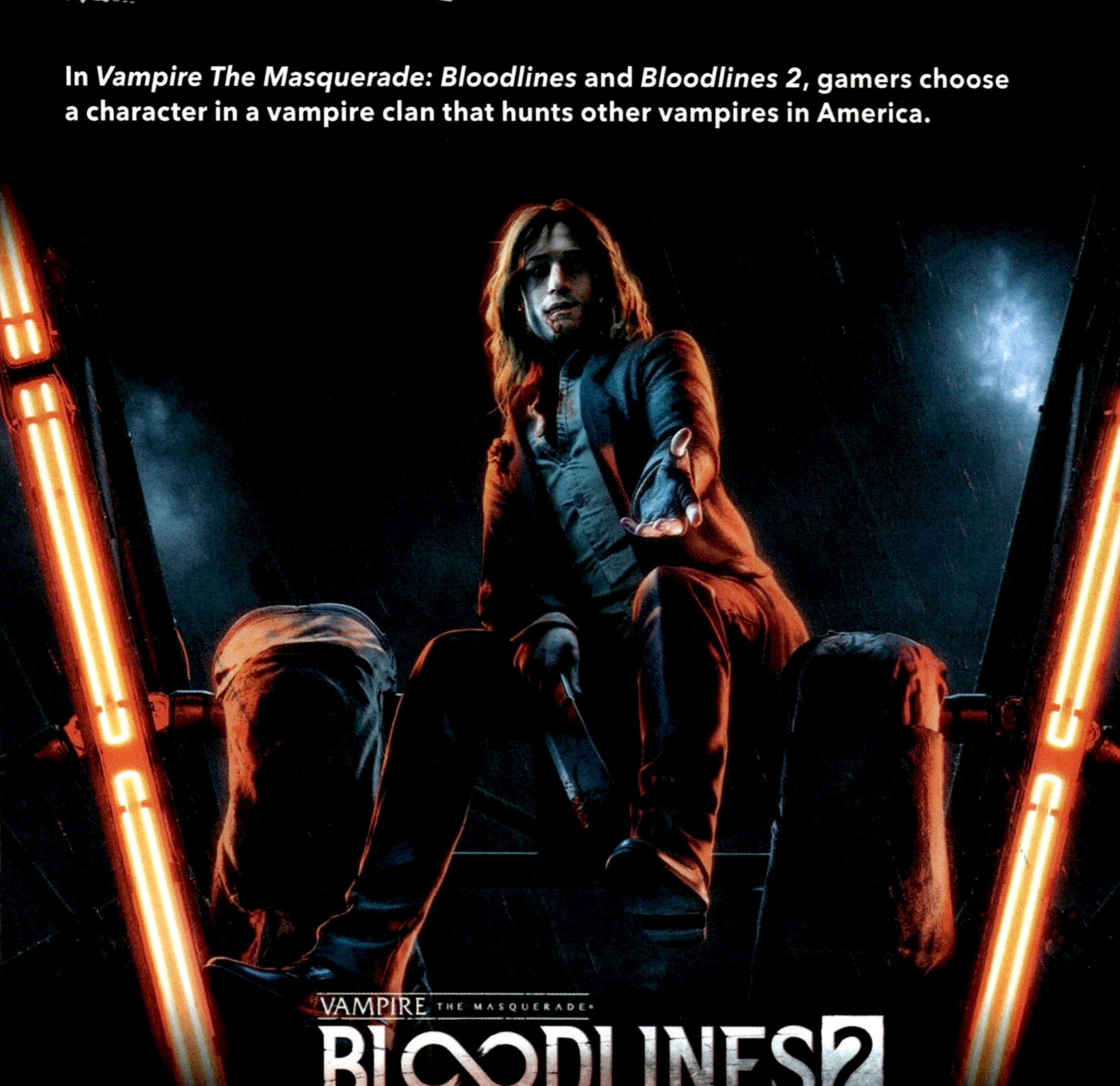

In *Vampire The Masquerade: Bloodlines* and *Bloodlines 2*, gamers choose a character in a vampire clan that hunts other vampires in America.

CHAPTER 9

Are Vampires Real?

Vampires are **mythical**, but people who tell tales of the **undead** make them seem quite real. Stories of vampires rising from their graves and draining humans of their blood have terrified people for generations.

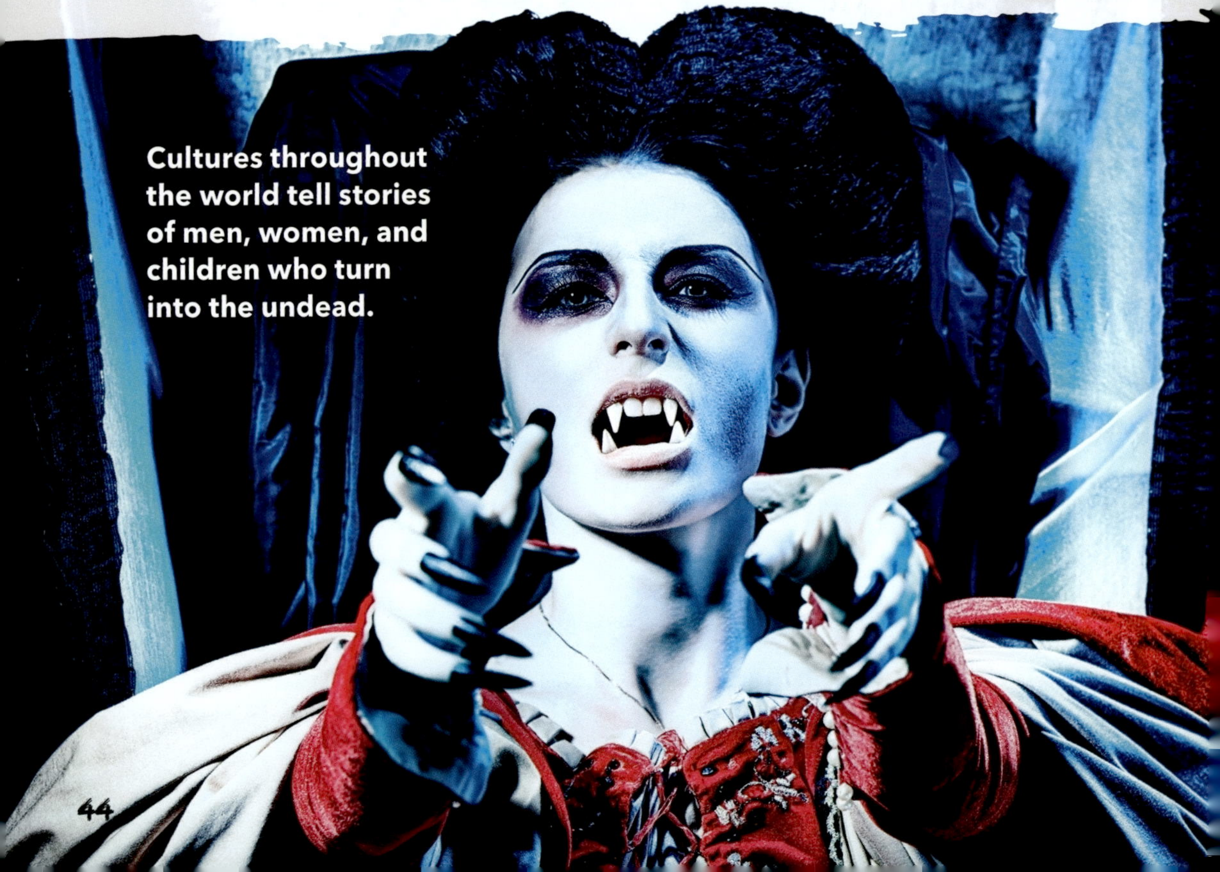

Cultures throughout the world tell stories of men, women, and children who turn into the undead.

XTREME Challenge

1) Besides bats, what are some other creatures that vampires are said to turn into?

2) According to legend, what are some ways a human can be turned into a vampire?

3) The term "nightmare" comes from what Austrian vampire?

4) Hopping vampires come from what country? Why do they hop?

5) What are some ways to kill a vampire?

6) In what country did the real Vlad Dracula live?

7) What medical conditions may make a person look like a vampire?

Glossary

curse – A series of words or a wish for something bad to happen to another person or thing.

decompose – To rot or decay. Usually, the tissue of once-living things, such as humans, animals, and plants, begins to decompose as soon as they die.

fiction – Stories that are made up by a writer or speaker. Not fact.

garlic – A strong-smelling bulb that looks somewhat like a small onion. Garlic is used in cooking and many medicines.

myth – A story that people once believed to be true. Myths often tell of the actions of gods, heroes, or supernatural beings with magical or extreme powers.

rabies – A disease caused by a virus that affects the central nervous system (brain and spinal cord) of mammals, including humans. Rabies causes excessive saliva, abnormal behavior, and eventual paralysis and death. People can get rabies when bitten or scratched by an infected wild or domestic animal.

recede – To move back.

Romania – A country in the southeastern part of Central Europe, roughly the size of Oregon.

talisman – A small object such as a stone, ring, or necklace, with magical powers. Some talismans are said to bring good luck, while others bring evil.

undead – The revived body of a dead person. The undead appear in many different forms such as vampires, ghosts, or zombies.

vile – Wicked or unpleasant to the extreme.

Online Resources

To learn more about the world's most vile vampires, please visit **abdobooklinks.com** or scan this QR code. These links are routinely monitored and updated to provide the most current information available.

Index